Crazy Poems
(The Ghosts)

Joseph Hart

Copyright© 2022 Joseph Hart
ISBN: 978-81-8253-865-8

First Edition: 2022
Rs. 200/-

Cyberwit.net
HIG 45 Kaushambi Kunj, Kalindipuram
Allahabad - 211011 (U.P.) India
http://www.cyberwit.net
Tel: +(91) 9415091004
E-mail: info@cyberwit.net

No part of this book may be reproduced or transmitted in any form or by any means, electronic, mechanical, photocopying, or otherwise, without the express written consent of Joseph Hart.

Printed at Repro India Limited.

inscribed to the memory of

John Keats

Contents

Tryst	9
Prayer	10
Urn	11
Mood	12
The Parthenon	13
Words	14
Morning Waking	15
Winter Happiness	16
Lines	17
Evening	18
Urn	19
Ebe	20
Storm	21
Endymion	22
A Place	23
The Castle	24
Ghosts	25
Sleep	26
Lines	27
Stranger	28
The Monk	29
A Jingle	30
Prevision Of Death	31
Lines	32
Consciousness	33
Winter Sleep	34
Four Short Poems	35
Squalor	36
Moment	37

Archaism	38
The Sleeper	39
Hallucination	40
The Perfect Place	41
Danny	42
Twilight	43
The Lions	44
The Fish	45
The Ghost	46
Alone	47
Sleep	48
Dreams	49
Short Poems	50
Short Poems	52
Short Poems	54
Night	56
A Thought	57
Memory	59
For Absolutely No One At All	60
Humanity	61
C.M.L.D.M.N.	62
Ghosts	63
Psychotic	64
The Phantom	65
J.T.	66
Elegy	67
Old	68
Dreams	69
Swimming	70
Psychosis	71
Worship	72
Reves	73
Lines Written In A Coffee Shop	74

Stanza On The Sea	75
Prescience Of Death	76
G.M.	77
Keats' Picture	78
The Sea	79
Unfinished	80
The Sea	81
"Il Tabarro"	82
6 a.m.	83
Crazy	84
Music	85
A Dream	86
Fragment	87
Keep	88
Verdi	89
The Skeleton	90
Chant	91
Memory	92
Defeat	93
Romance	94
Lines	95
Temperate Love	96
Written In Peace	97
Night Song	98
Left To Dreams	99
Keats	100
Innisfree	101
Rhythmed Beauty	102
Somewhere a cat	103
Anachronos	104
From A Rough Poem In Denny's	105
Verse	106
My Cat	107

Gaby	108
Alma	109
The Sea	110
Madness	111
"Shine"	112
Two Stanzas On Poetry	113
Two Stanzas	114
The Three Graces	115
Housman's Subject	116
My Death	117
Strangers	118
Analogy	119
Aristotle	120
Robin's Poem	121
Epitaph	122
Praise	123
Keats' Self	124
Picture	125
On The Ocean	126
The Temple	127
Rain	128
Defeat	129

Tryst

She nurtured her furious sadness
Deep, deep in luxurious madness.
Out of her eyes
Came the madness of lies.
Beneath which in deep melancholy
Overhung by green cypress and holly
She dwelt all alone
In a realm of her own
Adjudicating injustice with folly.

Her knight on his snorting white steed
Scattered dust as he galloped with speed
To the gate of her castle.
He sent off the vassal
Who guarded her door stiff and proper
In his clinking green armor of copper.
Then he ravished his maid
Who his kisses repaid
With such rush that he just couldn't stop her.

Prayer

God knows what I need.
Why must I ask him?
Millenniums of prayers
Must surely overtask him.

Worshiping their gods
In a cathedral or a tent,
They kiss the headman's hand
In its descent.

Christianity! It takes
Such awful strength to doubt it.
But if I were Aztec, I just
Wouldn't think about it.

Urn

On this urn there's guessless moods
And flowers uncompletely.
Glance-shown faces foster
Their behavior's explanation.
Thereupon the carved relief
Is smooth with shapes unmoving
Where the seeing of two eyes
Releases tensions slowly.
Water splashes from the urn
And wets the danceless structures.
Water in clear allegory
Floods the chiseled river.
Then darkness hides the situation
With the seer's sleep.

Mood

May I see only darkness,
Hear nothing except silence,
And may my feelings only feel the rain.
Then the explosions of the waves
On the placid rocks
Would themselves be forgetfulness.

The Parthenon

The soft curve of the Parthenon
Seems sincere to me.
My body is the structure of the building.
My soul, my happiness
Themselves are the sensation
That the structure's shape suggests.
I am the Parthenon, and it is me -
And in this instant I am beautiful.

Words

Nearer than the moon, the mist
Clothes with vacant amethyst
The naked empty fortress
Of the deep sea-shouldered dawn.
And through the columns I can see
The giant sun arise much like a fountain.

Morning Waking

Sleep-crushed like a wine-drenched urn
The morning marks us softly.
Briefly we relax and turn
As happily dawn happens.

Music softly echoes now
Through the doorless Parthenon.
Music soothes with knowing how.
Happiness is never done.

Soft we savor the embankment
Of the sleepy edge of earth
That near and distant musically
Makes a passing sense of worth.

Winter Happiness

Soft as the afternoon
On frosted windows
Warm as the tenderness
Of the fire burning
Deep as the afterglow
Of loved I couldn't know
Now is compared to snow
Like happiness sadly.

Slowly the warming cold
Fosters throughout me
Ages of infancy
Echoes of no where.
Trust swells like innocence
Grey rain like sad defense
Lantern-lit consequence
Deep, deep with beauty.

Lines

Above, the uninterpretable moon
Warm music out of sequence with events
A new permission from the Parthenon
The sun-shown outline of a face asleep
To hear enshaded under stoic trees
Human lullabies sung as you please
Are poems the prolegomena of sleep?
Who was Keats himself? How did he write?
What perfect eyes from ancient lore
See every wave toward the shore
And move it with a balanced myth
Unmasking what it's for?

Evening

The carnival evening opens for inspection
The free rose growing near the garden garden gate.
The spectre of the 12 o'clock of darkness
Breeds the fearful forest of the night.
The everlasting mercy of the sea
Nurses the sure promise when it weakens
That after just a few more human hours
Dawn will give night to forgetfulness.

Urn

A Grecian urn in bas-relief
Where purple wine will flow
And splash each flower, fern and leaf
Yet never let you know,
It drowns the elves their sleepy selves
Where they more softly go,
Though milky white and tender light
Lets every image show.
Around the edge a rambling hedge
Shades roses grey below,
And half a glimpse of rustic nymphs
Sheds music that I know.

Ebe

In her hand she holds the bowl that offers milk -
And from the darkness of her sleep she comes -
The statue Ebe.
She carries on her other side
The jug that has the milk she offers
And the texture of the statue is as softly white
As the milk she offers -
From her downward look, her balanced stance
And the long relaxing
Drapery of sleep her body wears.

Storm

Trees succumb to other brushing trees
Deeply windswept rain and darkness swirl
And sudden thunder rumbles everywhere.
Five seconds then the shriveled hand of lightning
Whose large and icy branches in explosion
Briefly give the night a stranger day.
And now the moon behind a pool of clouds,
A circle among shadows, slept in sleep.
The dull enduring evidence of night
Infiltrates the house above the sea
Where it's settled in untroubled sleep -
A giant Sphinx beside the summer night.
The Parthenon in deep and tender darkness
On a cliff above the crashing ocean.
Inside the house there's music, warmth and meaning,
While outside in the storm there's perfect time.

Endymion

Fairer than Mnemosyne
And softer than a sigh
Tenderer than history
Upon a native eye.
Gentle and attendant shadows
Follow on the path
The sprawling ivy takes
And underneath an arbor
Endymion awakes.

A Place

A violent summer sky
Shook by instinctive thunder
The dinosaur of sleep
Drowsing underneath a shade
Deep in an afternoon repose
Permission - go to sleep.
The proper river flows,
A quiet lullaby,
Into a barren glade
Where an infant lies asleep, asleep.

The Castle

The rocky cold dawn-dominated castle
Is heroic in the earthy sky.
Age-emptied cypress stumps in staunch defense
Gently lean as if for new support
Against the stone-bound castle in the fog,
As if in a sleep-protected dream.
I can press my hand upon a wall
Rock and rough and rising out of sight.
This castle seems much like a god to me.
Ledges made each of rock-wonder stairs
Cramped and circling rise inside the towers
Where small square windows overlook the grass
And the wide and green expanse of purple flowers,
Made human by the emblem of the dawn,
And leaves rustling together
In a parliamentary splendor.
The purple bolt that drapes the grey austere
Falls in slow melancholy downward slopes,
While outside in historical grey darkness
Tons of wind explode against the walls.

Ghosts

A sleepy description
Of ghostly affairs -
A candle,
A seance at midnight
In a yellow-lit room
By a lantern
Where the dismal make prayers
To the gloom.
The house in decay
Is in ruins permitting
The traffic of ghosts
In and throughout it -
A vagrant remembrance
That random occurs
In an old personality
Gone to the sea.
And outside, the ocean
Leaves suds on the shore
And makes magical music
Throughout the old house
With its roar.

Sleep

I am seeping through the casement
Of a disenchanted sleep
Universally beloved
For its warm neutrality.
And a ghost of smoke is curling
Through the window in the air.
And far away and soothing
I can feel and hear the ocean.
It's in poesy that oceans
Have more meaning than the sea.

Lines

The candle smoke is rising
Through an infinite geometry,
And I am slowly yielding
To the guardian of sleep,
The soft caretaker, sleep.

1967

Stranger

I stare into a stranger's face
Until it is familiar,
Until I am at home.
But strangers leave,
And strangers pass
And there is no way home
Except in memory.

The Monk

The monk slept in his coffin
In the monastery dim,
A bastion against a deeper warmth.
The chilly weather, wan
Was cloudy, overcast.
The water turned to ice beside the door.
The morning was so grey,
The greyness went so deep
That dawn seemed warm to see, to see: to touch.
The monk slept in his coffin
In the greyness of the vault.
The flowers froze and withered on their stems.
The castle of the monastery,
Rocks upon each other piled
Was suited to the morning, wet and grey
And cold as oceans underneath the swells.
The monk slept in his coffin
While the early morning froze
And remnants of the disappearing night
Dissipated in the dismal dawn.

6-2-85

A Jingle

A poem is a penny's worth
Of what I want to feel.
And sleep itself can make a thing
Seem absolutely real.

The starry night I do not see,
But only see my sleeping,
To see: to feel: to touch. At dawn
Where are the dreams for keeping?

The shore of sand the ocean waves
Will swallow up completely.
So sleep will swallow up a dream,
Or dreams the sleep and sweetly.

6-3-85

Prevision Of Death

While sitting in a coffee shop
Beside a cup of coffee
I watched my consciousness become extinct.
I projected it before me
Like a mirror on the wall,
Or an object in the mirror,
Or an image without shape
And saw it disappear and cease to be.

Lines

I'll conjure up a little sheaf of verses
For anyone to browse among and cull
Some paradoxes for a winter day.
And sleep is half the pleasure of a dream.
Sepulchral night becomes a perfect day
Wherein I see the shapes I had suspected
When it was dark. As sleep falls from my form
I make some sense of what I apprehend.
But I could be a mystic or a monk
Among the ghosts and without any god.
Half forgotten dreams are half remembered
As things suggest the dreams I half recall.

Consciousness

I can feel the gentle flower
Intersecting with its image
In my brain.
And suddenly I feel
The subtle masturbation
Of my mental senses
By the tender flower
Colorful and fragrant.
My soul informs my body.
And a consciousness of time is everything.
And the evening like a Sphinx
Has settled on the shaggy grass.
Can I remember what I never touched?

Winter Sleep

The rain is dripping soft as sleep
Upon the window pane.
The night is here. And sleep itself
Is summoning itself.
The blankets underneath my chin
Are proof against the cold.
And once again my body's heat
Has warmed my burrow, made my bed
A safe, a summer cloud.
Some shadows move about the room
Like ghosts inside a castle,
Archaic squares of solid stone
Less permanent it seems than this,
The shadow of my sleepy room
Upon the edge of darkness,
That shimmers in incipient sleep,
Ephemeral and fixed.

Four Short Poems

Out of the gaslight of ended existence
Emerges a rhythm of courts and kings.
Hamlet gesticulates madly, more madly
Ignoring Ophelia who's dying alone.

1966

To hallucinate a lover
On my skin and to awaken
In the arms of love's embraces
Is the sweetest dream of all.

Let's christen a ghost in a church that is old,
Archaic, decaying and stone,
Where the sea breezes float
Through the ruins and moat,
And all music relaxes in time.

To hold a person whom I love
But never feel his kiss!
Happiness flees like a dream
And leaves me only this:
A poem made of nothingness.
Nothingness is bliss.

1997

Squalor

Read my poems when you're drunk
Because they will make sense then.
In your intoxication
You will see their lovely truths
And tender depths.
My poems have the magic
Of total human worthlessness.
And there's a deep and subtle rhapsody
In such self-disregard.
And anyone who hates himself
Without an ecstasy
Cannot believe in gods
Or other myths.

Moment

The Keats lay on the table while I slept.
And it was in the room
While I was sound asleep.
The Keats lay closely by me while I slept.
And all the night was darkness.
The Keats could not be read,
Nor even seen, nor I inside the room.
There was a gentle touch
In this propinquity.
The Keats lay on the table while I slept.
A ghost of silence grew
In this proximity,
Although no barrier was there
Except the sleepy darkness.
The Keats lay on the table while I slept.
In magical awareness
While I was unaware,
The Keats lay on the table while I slept.

7-16-85

Archaism

Be brave, my child!
Be brave and dream.
Be brave but never carve
Your fantasies in rock
Forevermore.
Let them form and dissipate
As sleeping goes away
At dawn. And then be there
To dream again.
So dream in hardiment, my son.
But even cowards dream

2-20-85

The Sleeper

He was asleep.
He felt my gaze.
He woke and looked at me.
Nor did he dream
My gaze into a dream
And thus defend
His sleep against intrusion.
He was asleep.
I looked at him.
My stare upon his skin
Awoke him from
The slumber of his dreams.

6-22-85

Hallucination

I was living in a jerrybuilt,
Moldy old motel
With only just a bedroom and a door.
In a sense it was a home
But only in the sense
That any place would do as well as none.
I was sitting on the bed
And I was looking at the corner
And I heard a ringing in my ears.
And then I saw myself
Tangible and clear
Sitting in the corner in a chair.
Distinct, this apparition
Looked toward the bed
Where I was sitting. And I looked at him.
It was myself I saw. And we were there.
I whispered to the image
To come closer to the bed
Where we'd have sex together, he and I.
I lusted for this phantom
That I deeply craved to touch.
It slowly, very slowly disappeared.
Dim around the edges
And transparent in the middle,
When I spoke it slowly disappeared.
Then at last I only saw
The corner and the chair.

1972/1985

The Perfect Place

Were this not such a precipice
So awesome and sublime
And grand above a sea that bursts below,
Explodes against the ragged rock
Abutments as they climb
And finish where the fragrant mosses grow;
Were this not such a living, dead
And natural chateau
With flowers nodding in the breeze
And shade of double-branching trees
Gloomy in the sunniest of days
Where no sheep graze;
Could I not hear the shadows
Of the thunder of the waves
Lointain while looking at a purple sky
All mixed with cloudy grey,
Both near and far away -
I would not think it half so rich to die,
In willing acquiescence fling my body from the edge
Of this auspicious ledge
And hit the sea! Not half so rich to die.

7-2-85

Danny

Danny seemed so very sad
So very long ago.
That's all that I
Remember of him now.
Did I know more
When I was close to him?
A concept: grief,
His shape was sad
And was with sadness filled.
That's all that I remember of
His smokey faceless image.
Did I love him then?
I love him now.
Does this love occur in retrospect?
He was warm
And he was fond of me.
I remember Danny long ago.

6-12-85

Twilight

I don't want to fall asleep and fall
Into the hole where nothingness exists
With nothing but the night to cover me.
I want to stay awake and to defy
This drowsiness that's coming over me.
I want to stay awake and so to live
Among the many objects I enjoy,
Not plunge into some solipsistic dreams,
And swim unknown among fantastic dreams.

The Lions

The dawn-lighted rock is rough and steep,
And windy thunder breaks against the walls.
Mammoth lions guard the largest portals
Marking with their sandy stoic posture
Huge smooth windblown manes around their faces
Beautiful and awesome in the darkness,
Colorless, stone-colored, appearing real
Structured out of rock and lion shapes
Forelegs firm against the formless earth
Rock-strewn, sprouting random sparse-branched bushes,
Calm, serenely gazing, self-assured
Over the spare barren countryside.
Darkened by the shaded vestibule
Of the castle's gate-door's massive arcs
Shaped like two hands cupped into an alcove
Inset where two stony lions stand,
Wrapping their long tails around their haunches
Where they rest. Their undisturbing stare
Showing soothing strength so calmly spoken
More normal and more human than the Sphinx,
Specific, with the same authority.

The Fish

If god created paradise
For only you and me,
Why did he put fishes
At the bottom of the sea?
Why did he make the dinosaur?
Why did he make the flea?
And why should I imagine
(I just ask for what it's worth)
That god will do in heaven
What he never did on earth?

The Ghost

A ghost about this custom haunts
Doing darkly what it wants,
Unaware and so unfeared,
Alone about the midnight weird.
The passing bell that rings its toll
While melancholy oceans roll
Again, again will sound its knell
While wave-surmounting breakers swell.
Who was this ghost? And what is he
That frequents cobwebs and the sea?
And can this dead phantom pass
Through walls of rock like light through glass?
Oh spirit from the grave set free,
Would I were you and you were me!

1-10-98

Alone

Exquisitely and happily alone,
Exceeding pleasure courses through my body
And I'm aware of not a thing but this.
Puccini's rich and soaring tunes
And deeper orchestrations
Isolate me in a dream of joy.
The gentle passages of Keats or Brooke
Alienate the world around my room
And leave me there alone with what I feel,
Abandoned to my sentiments alone -
As in his sleep the dreamer is alone -
And sleep is half the pleasure of a dream.

Sleep

The sleepy little jerk before you sleep,
The cat-like
Twitching of a finger or a hand
Involuntary is, and so is sleep.
I love to see you lie in comfort soothing
With every muscle tenseless, unoppressed.
I want to see you calm in your repose,
And every now and then pretend or sense
That a movement is a movement in a dream,
Or else your body on the verge of waking
Has shuddered and returned itself to sleep -
Like water that's about to overflow
The edges of a glass, but then relaxes
Back into the greater mass below.

Dreams

Talk while I'm asleep and I will weave
Your voice into the fabric of a dream.
Or contrawise, suppose I had a dream
That I was walking through a misty fog
And went across some wet and dewy grass,
And when I woke, my sheets were damp and cold
And there were footprints going to my bed.
Or wished so hard that there were ghosts about,
That ghosts appeared and ate me in a bite!

Short Poems

A mixture of murders and gods,
Of horrors and saints -
I looked over the edge of the earth
And saw the eternal void -
Ugly, dark, abysmal, charred and smoky,
Horrifying, terrifying, sad...

Because a person doesn't talk
Back when he's insulted
Does not imply in any sense
That he believes he's wrong.

I tumbled over the edge of sleep
Into darkness.
I don't remember
What I discovered there.
And then I heard
The morning urgently calling.
And midnight was gone.

I'm home again at last -
I'm writing poems,
Some songs that sound
The bottom of my soul
And surface bearing dreams
Just half asleep.

I sing of the immortal grave
To which we all incline.
Among blasphemies and roses,
We'll sleep. And sleep is fine.

When I awoke this morning
I recalled a dream
That had a little sleep
Still sticking to it.

Short Poems

I lie in bed and wait until
My thoughts disintegrate, until
Soft sleep subdues my body
With its warm totality,
It's deep neutrality.

When did I fall asleep?
I don't remember.
What did I dream
The first time that I slept?

When I become one with my dreams
And sleeping is being sincere,
I'll never walk out of my house,
And never want anyone near.

Less long-lived than a dream
When one awakes,
That melts in the warmth of awareness
Like snowflakes -

Why do I dream
Such dreams so complex
Filled with colors and meaning and sounds
Just to forget them at dawn?

His bed unkempt,
The dreamer dreamt.
And while he slept
A tryst he kept,
And never woke again.

When you imply
I must infer.
What Roger was
I wish I were.

Short Poems

Let him rest - by sleep possessed -
Sleep-blessed - unknown and unexpressed -
What are the dreams he can expect
Where sleep and waking intersect?
Let sleep its sovereignty extend.
Sleep: a prelude. Sleep: the end.

We fell asleep embracing.
We woke embracing still.
I wish that I were with you.
I think I always will.

After he had summoned up
A dream out of the sea
And made the universe, - this deity,
What did he then?
He caused himself
Not ever to have been.

I loved you all unknowing and unknown.
You were too beautiful,
I was afraid.
I wondered who you were
And whence you came.
You went away
But nonetheless
At last I know your name.

Pococurante, the sea
Once was the mother of me.
There in the fog and the mist
By the waves and the swells I was kissed.
Nurtured and warm
By a storm on the sand,
I was given my form
By a hand
From the soul of the sea.

Night

When I am subdued by sleep
I see
A photograph of a psyche.
This is me.

Close removed
From daylight's cogitation
I see things
In night's imagination.

Perhaps I'll dream
If all the stars are right
Of your warm smile,
A candle in the night.

1974

A Thought

I was sitting at a table
With my forearm on the surface,
And I saw the objects near me
And I felt the things I saw.
The typewriter was blue
And with nausea and love
I saw it. And the table
Square, impermeable, hard.
The flowers on the table,
In the living room the sofa,
And the windows, and the edge of
The piano in the room
I saw, and felt in sensing.
In this consciousness contentment.
And I heard the traffic passing
Out of doors. And it was evening
So as usual the cars
Seemed to make a sound of darkness.
Then I saw
A photograph of Keats
On the edge of the piano
And it was a hard sensation
Unresembling all the others,
In a sense, another thing.
For the photograph had meaning
That was personal to me.
And for a moment I believed that I

Would rather see the paper
That the photograph had come in,
Sent from London long ago.

2-27-85

Memory

My nephew offered me a can
While he was still in diapers.
I remember still
But he does not.
What thought (distinct, amorphous)
Occupied his brain
And prompted him to offer me a can?
Now far away and out of reach
Is his memory of this
If memory there was,
That I remember yet.

For Absolutely No One At All

My love - he is a gentle thing
My perfect-hearted love
And he
Reminds me of a flower
Rooted soft in breath or sleep
Or life
But in my love
I think there moves
A moment of the sea
My love is a treasure when he talks
To me
In silliness or in sincerity
And when he's happy
My love's beautiful
Sad, perhaps
He's possibly profound
I want to see him sad
But gentle love
Be happy nonetheless
My love - he is a gentle thing
My perfect-hearted love

12/82

Humanity

How many Shostakoviches
Are dead in Yugoslavia?
How many Brookes
Lie buried in mass graves?
How many with the genius
Potential of John Keats
Rot unrealized in Africa?

8-30-98

C.M.L.D.M.N.

Cathie walks the beaches
Of ridged and crumbling sands.
What the ocean teaches
Cathie understands.

And when she walks the sidewalks
She never maunders slow.
She says she tries to walk as if
She has somewhere to go.

1965/1998

Ghosts

A poem is a ghost
And it can pass through walls.
It can wander corridors
Of dusty dismal halls
By only candlelight.
A poem is a ghost
That relishes the grave,
A troglodyte defunct
Who paints upon his cave
By only candlelight.
A poem is a ghost
By a magician made
Of paradox and images.
It's magic that's displayed
By only candlelight.
A poem is a ghost
A seance of the soul
That conjures up fey phrases
Come altogether whole
By only candlelight.
A poem is a ghost
By sleeping deified
That haunts the old unconscious
An id transmogrified
By only candlelight.

9-28-98

Psychotic

When I was psychotic
I saw as a child -
Everyone was beautiful
And nobody was bad.
And everything was magical
And everything was strange.
Although I didn't sweat
I had an acrid smell
Whose pungency I savored
But of which I was ashamed.
Everything was symbols
And irony. And meanings
Implied but never stated
Drove me underground.
I lived in two dimensions -
One of common understanding,
One that went unspoken.
And in agony and horror
I thought what seemed to me
Would never coincide with what was said.

The Phantom

A ghost is at the window,
A ghost is at the door,
A little bit of something
That now is nevermore.
The rain falls in the flowers.
The rain falls on the shore.
The rain falls on the vestige
Of what is nevermore.
At night I see the candles
Of stars that were before
But now are dead and dark,
Extinct forevermore.
I think a ghost asleep
Can hear no ocean roar,
But instead is double-dead
And twice is nevermore.

10/98

J.T.

There he sleeps, his arms outspread
Across a rumpled morning bed.
And to my eyes he seems to be
Just on the verge of memory
With nothing unsaid.

Unseeing although seen by me
He sleeps in greater liberty.
And every dream inside his head
Is a book I never read,
An unheard melody.

How can this prince of consciousness
So beautifully bless
His countenance with tenderness
And consequently dress
His perfect nakedness
With such exquisite harmony
Upon a rumpled bed?

1972

Elegy

My poesy is all my life is worth.
Dead gods dethroned
Lie darkling in dank tombs.
My consciousness embosks
Old loves among dim shadows
As though in vagrant flowers -
They're gone and half forgotten.
Have they forgotten me?
They must have done,
It's been so many years.
When my life is over
I will leave no legacy
Except perhaps the poems that I wrote.

1-18-98

Old

With a sad deep sense of horror
She watched herself grow old.
Both puzzled and bewildered
She saw the metamorphosis
From nothingness to nothingness -
As night deposes day,
As dawn displaces sleep,
Ineluctable and bad.

Dreams

The cryptic obfuscating
Honesty of dreams!
When phantoms recognizable
And ghosts come out to browse!
Darkling and benighted
I wake in early dawn
And question what I dreamt
The night before.

5-22-98

Swimming

In the currents of the ocean,
Buffeted about by water,
Made to move by moving tides
And waves and swells and breakers,
He missed his sleep,
Salubrious and soothing
Met kindly with the memory of dreams.
The sea was cold.
A tender dream is warm.
The sea is brine, a cavern full of tears.
But good sleep smiles
And with its dreams
Both kisses and caresses.
I wish I were asleep in dreams -
New dreams, old dreams, some repetitious,
Whose wholeness mimics all the heartless sea.

6-19-98

Psychosis

His psychosis went away
As unobserved as breathing,
As imperceptibly as drifting
Silently to sleep.
He did not see it going,
Only noticed it was gone,
And never knew
When it had ceased to be.
The horror that had haunted him,
The dreaming unasleep,
Except in memory was as
If it never was.
The horror and the magic and the love.

6-24-98

Worship

I killed god. I worshiped him to death
Just to feel his blood wash over me.
And it was through my humility
That I was exalted in his place.
Reverence it was that catapulted
Me into his sphere, onto his throne.
And there I breathed his air and felt his pulse
In a rhapsody of non-communication.
Why not?
Should I lie bloodless by the altar
On the cold stone floor of a cathedral
I could not have made,
Care for a god that I can not imagine,
And dwell in darkness and catastrophe?

Reves

My dreams make sense when I'm asleep.
They don't when I'm awake.
Awake, asleep - dichotomy.
I understand my dreams when I'm asleep.
But they are enigmatic when I wake.
So what is understanding?
What's to understand?
What is the understanding of a dream?
Why do dreams make sense to me
When in my sleep I dream them?
Why don't I comprehend them when I wake?

4-4-87

Lines Written In A Coffee Shop

The melancholy ocean
Much more wistful than the sea
Summons up the spectres
With its haunted symmetry
Until every grave is empty
And the moon is very low.
Across the gentle sand
Some gentle breezes start to blow.
I perceive a rose appearing
In the twilight dim and nearing.
With a crimson scent endearing
It has found a place to grow.
Here there is no tidal thunder
For the thief of poesy
To plunge into and plunder
In a human rhapsody
Of excommunication.
I remember and I feel.
But this sensive celebration
Or this passive incantation
Is sincere but isn't real.

6-21-86

Stanza On The Sea

I enjoy to sit and watch the sea.
I can become the ocean
In paradox and harmony
And with a faint devotion
But with a deep emotion.
The curling waves, they lick the shore
Ere swallowed by the sea.
But deafening, the ocean's roar
Is musical to me.
I hear it tenderly.

3-1-87

Prescience Of Death

The legitimate sadness of Atheism,
The honest horror of death
Nullifies encumbrances of thought
And leaves the soul dissatisfied
With poesy and sleep -
And leaves the soul alone upon the shore
To stare toward the everlasting sea.
And reasoned out of reason
It's aye misunderstood.

3-8-87

G.M.

The shades were drawn.
The lights were out.
The darkness had no odor.
We settled down to sleep
While in each other's arms.
I don't remember when I went to sleep.
Throughout the night, the dismal night
In that eternal chasm
Called sleep
We slept together in each other's arms.
And in the morning when we woke
We were hugging still.
Impressed you were in love,
But I was angry.

Keats' Picture

I gaze upon my photograph of Keats.
It makes me warm and nourishes my mind.
A solid gaze against a gentle face,
The contact of his visage and my eyesight
Becomes at once a deep and warm rapport
Invisible that's nearly physical,
A ghost that I can stick my fingers through.
It isn't that his look looks far away,
But that the look is Keats'. It isn't that
His head is even, strong, symmetrical,
But that the head is Keats. Yet it may be
That these fair things endear it more to me.

The Sea

The tireless repetition of the sea
Send its wholesome whisper of a hush
Toward, across the everlasting shore
In a rush. Occasional the gulls
Like stars intrude the darkness of the sounds.
The tireless repetition of the sea
Untrite, unhackneyed, fresh, forever new
As the sempiternal starting of the day
Is ever solemn, joyous and alone.
Abandoned as the shells it casts ashore,
Magnificent in its indifference,
It seems to warm me as if we were known.
There's inspiration in remembering
The ocean that I saw once long ago,
A tender deep afflatus like the sea
That gives the shore primeval tenderness.

Unfinished

As warm and gentle as the wind
That takes the ships to sea
So is the ghost that half-chagrined
By daylight comes to me.
I reach my fingers through the ghost
But touch as nothing touches.
Believe the heart that clutches!
In the distance I can see
The ocean lap its rhapsody
Upon the shore, alone and free.
It's half enough to comfort me.
What could I write but what I wrote?
Or write but what I do?
This subtle sea is so remote,
Each single wave of little note
For eyes defunct asleep to dote
Upon forever new.
A single self informs my soul
And gives my body shape.
Dreams that I do not control
Frequently escape.

6-7-86

The Sea

Dead men watch the sea!
With eyes all fixed and sightless
They stare beyond the shore
And see the waves in harmony
Overcome each other there.
Dead men watch the sea!
What do waves give dead men's eyes?
As tide succumbs to tide,
As swell takes over swell
The surf that nourishes the shore
Did not bring my heart to me.
When earth is ended and the sky's
Extinguished like a candle flame,
What becomes of dead men's eyes?
Dead men watch the sea!

6-16-86

"Il Tabarro"

In "Il Tabarro" Puccini conjures up
An everlasting aural
Image of a river in a fog.
Profoundly felt like sleep or poesy,
It seems that I am standing on the wharf
Myself enfolded in the sober mist

2-8-86

6 a.m.

This morning when I crossed the road
From home to have some coffee
At 6 a.m. the sky was black and grey
And purple, and the darkness seemed
To add a new dimension
To ones already known.
Grey is shallow. But this grey
Was deep, as deep as death.
The sky was purple underneath
The clouds that didn't move
Their broken bulks, like chunks of earth.
The sky was beautiful.

11-18-85

Crazy

In a shadowy sense,
My mind split.
The room was filled with colors.
They surrounded and involved me.
It was warm,
Despite the pain.
I puked colors.
The room was small
And dark.
It was evening.
The lights were dim.

9-26-91

Music

The hush of sleep was in the night.
His way was lit by candlelight.
The hem of his robe dragged on the ground.
He gently moved without a sound.
With shadows behind and shadows before
He slowly opened the old oak door.
Heavily on its hinges hung
The door that with a whisper swung
Open. In its wooden frame
He stood and let his candle flame.
The flame was steady. No draft or gust
Disturbed the candle or the dust.
He walked into the dim-lit gloom
And stood inside the music room.
Warm and open, wise with joy
In worlds that time cannot destroy,
He felt, inhaled sweet music's noise
In a mystic's circle's equipoise.

1-24-90

A Dream

Last night I had a lovely dream
That all throughout the day
I've kept about to touch,
But out of grasp.
Deep inside my body
I can feel the dream as yet,
And kept some glimpses
Taken from the night.
I wish tonight
To dream it all again -
Or even a continuance of it.

11-17-89

Fragment

Do all sensations pass?
And is sensation like a shadow?
A memory of freedom in new sleep!
Deeply sleeping tender shadows
Like sensations touch my face
On the other side of darkness and despair.
And a boat upon the water
Like a shadow on my senses
Allows old sleep to fill its sails,
And moves toward no other
Than a sea-soaked wooden harbor,
And beaches on awakefulness and dawn.

1-23-90

Keep

I shall build a castle out of sleep
(A fortress mighty as a cobweb is)
In which I'll hide the treasures of my life -
Gone faces that my heart remembers still,
Old feelings that I'm able to indulge,
Kafka, Junkets, Donizetti, Proust.

Verdi

When Verdi exhales thunder
Old heaven disappears
And other heavens come
To take its place.

11-23-89

The Skeleton

The skeleton has stretched a string
Among his body's bones,
Fastened it and made it taut.
He plucks the cord and makes it sing,
Elicits an array of tones -
Sensations, feelings, thoughts.
And thus he makes himself
The subject of his songs.

Chant

Such coruscating ecstasy
To live alone beside the sea
Inditing lucid poesy
Agreeable and warm -
To summon up a fantasy
Of words that seem to sense and see
And tell in all their minstrelsy
A meaning that is warm -
To live alone in jealousy
Of this alive colossal sea,
Free in my apostasy
And reasonably warm -

Memory

An actor must rehearse his lines for days
To memorize the character he plays.
Yet a phrase or incident befalls
That evermore the memory recalls.

3-14-86

Defeat

I'm a person too.
If they don't know that
By now
There's nothing
I can tell them.

Romance

A poem read by candlelight
In an empty castle
Cold but by the grating
In a small rock chamber,
Read to rhythms perfectly,
Allow the syllables
To make their music -
Pictures in the air
And human phrases -
Narcissistic songs.

Lines

Unforced sleep falls over me -
A wave across the shore.
Comparing slumber to the sea!
A perfect metaphor!

Beneath the tide lie dreams and reefs
And hulls of sunken ships,
Forgotten loves and old beliefs
And unremembered lips.

Temperate Love

Sleep not in sunlight too intense
Nor in the forest grimly dense
But in the shadow of a tree
With dark, warm, gentle light on thee,
And all with no philosophy
But love and sad mortality.
And I shall lie with thee my friend
If thou dost want it til the end
Of daylight. Know the night with me
In sleep and gentle ecstasy.
Our passing thoughts we shall exchange.
No trait in thee will seem more strange
To me than those that are mine own.
And safer love we've never known.

Written In Peace

All I want to do is pace the floor
And be lonely - that is what I'm for -
Writing verse describing what I feel
In phrases artificial, rather real
While listening to music in the gloom
Of the shadows of my empty room.
Am I happy? Yes, I think I am.
I am no one. I don't give a damn.
I never cussed in verse when I was young.
I was proper. Now my song is sung.
When I'm happy, I forget (eschew?)
All the pain my feelings ever knew
If any. Somehow I can rise above
Scuttled ships and unrequited love.

Night Song

In the dark transparent midnight air
All the earth is quiet, and I stare.
Summer's ending and the night is cool,
But the days are hot. The moon's a jewel
Large and broken, dangling among stars
In clouds that drift like huge thalassic bars.
Time passes to time past. Memories spurn
The hope however warm that they'll return.
A cat, a bed, closed sleepy eyes, a yawn.
A deed remembered is a deed that's gone.

Left To Dreams

Left to dreams I write old poetry
Made new by present sense. The sea anoints
The sitter on the beach who hears the waves
Penetrate his fantasies asleep
With beauty which can substitute for truth.
The truth is everywhere. And feelings go
Deep, and feelings register the truth.

Keats

I remember someone
Underneath a tree
Sitting on a lawn
Reading Keats to me.

A memory apocryphal
From long ago I note
As showing more to me
In verse than what I wrote.

Following came Swinburne,
Matthew Arnold, men
Who've faded into time.
I was 20 then.

Innisfree

I shall go to Innisfree
Where no one's heard of pain
And death comes like a memory
To soothe the sadly sane,

Where despair is forsaken
And fantasies find fulfilling
And sensation can be taken
When it's ready, warm and willing.

Say that to Innisfree I went
And didn't say goodbye,
Where nothing means more than sleep has meant
Beneath a summer sky.

Though I could poem history
And conjure each Plantagenet
I cannot describe Innisfree
Because I can't imagine it.

Rhythmed Beauty

I agree completely with Poe -
Rhythmed beauty, a matter of taste.
I shall pick up the candle and go
Out of the country he left in waste.
Ghouls and spectres. As sad as death.
Meter was never my bailiwick.
I'm better at rhythm. It comes like breath.
A team of dogs driven by a stick.

Somewhere a cat

Somewhere a cat
Rubs its side against a fence.
That's sleep.
Cobwebs between doorless jambs
Are doors.
That's the moon.
Dark purple wine
Splashes down the sides
Of a lead mug.
That's the night.

Anachronos

All sensations pass;
And so do gods.
A sacred book unread
Will be forgotten,
And all its verities
Exist no more.
But sleep will fill the gaps of time;
And dinosaurs reborn
May thunder like a mountain on the earth
Or bellow like an ocean in the trees.

3-26-85

From A Rough Poem In Denny's

An open wound, raw,
Walked upon by spiders -
The Phoenix with assistance
Rises from a grave -
Poets in disturbances
Compose between the bullets -
Chaos and insanity!
I need a quiet place,
A loneliness - Brer Rabbit in
The thicket and the briars -
Discovering today that absolutely
Jordan likes me
(All things notwithstanding) -
Being happy not because,
In spite of other people -

6-17-11

Verse

There's more to verse than meter.
There is also less.
Structure is a talent,
Poetry a guess.

My Cat

I pet my cat. He shuts his eyes,
In sleepy warm contentment lies.
In my house he's not a waif
And thinks he is completely safe.
Precious cat, you make me cry.
You're no more secure than I.

Gaby

Gaby! Like a sun, the northern star
Luminously glowing, shines in Denny's -
Her fearless individuality
Radiates a human happiness
That when she smiles -
Makes my heart smile as well -
And when she is distracted or displeased
And doesn't smile - my attitude feels dark,
The room is darker in comparison -
An Indian raised on a reservation
Who left home the day she was allowed
To be free - Her happiness is freedom -
To release the bondage of my soul -

6-1-11

Alma

Burning coals and embers - like a flame -
So the cap of hair upon your head -
With a heart that nobody will tame -
Truth! Like something I have only read -
Slender and diminutive and small -
Spoken like a sailor in a squall -
No gods or angels in your firmament -
Nonetheless as though from heaven sent -
A rapier that's capped - but quick the tongue -
Alma! May you stay forever young!

6-20-11

The Sea

The ocean is an ugly thing.
You drown in its embrace.
From its depths you don't escape
In animal disgrace.

You like a sunken galleon sink
And settle in the silt,
Investigated by the fish,
Eyes closed. Do what thou wilt.

And as the currents carry you
Beneath the sea and far,
You are extinguished like a lamp,
And buried, like a star.

Madness

He's weak minded. Actually he's strong.
I'm weak minded. Like a leaky faucet.
Why should I say "sadly" when the night
Empty of all stars is threatening
To engulf the two of us together?
That's not sadness. That is Frigidaire.
Nature (or our parents) did us in
All overseen by some dead deity.
He sits alone and laughs. And in my car
While driving I shout wantonly and cuss,
And in perfect phrases execrating,
Triumph over all who vanquished me.

"Shine"

I sit alone upon the beach.
Thalassic thunder rolls.
The ocean whispers to the fog,
"Madmen have no souls."

But if they do have hearts and souls
(In ruins and in tatters),
They wander by the sea and ask,
"Whatever really matters?"

Madmen are not brave,
But cowardly and wrong,
Seldom make much sense,
And are not loved for long.

Two Stanzas On Poetry

To come up with the something that is art -
Rhythms, rhymes and images and phrases -
The truths that come to those who live apart -
Inconsequential truths - and that amazes

The mental senses - like a single tone
Sung by a soprano singing high -
Or the ocean to a man who lives alone
Who sings to it to hear the sea reply -

Two Stanzas

In a world ephemeral and bleak,
Evanescent as a rainy day,
I unearthed a treasure that endures,
Old, archaic, desultory, fey.

It's you that I discovered in my dig -
Youthful, fair - not swathed in bands and tatters,
From an archaeology of sleep,
Something more than poetry that matters.

The Three Graces

The oak has split and acts as braces
For the flowers it displaces
And the three reclining Graces
Seated in their balanced posture
In this cool and blue-green cloister.
Rich and fragrant flowers wreathe them,
And a river runs beneath them.
One watches her reflection
In still extro-introspection.
The other two relax conversing
While the morning sun is nursing
Deep wide shadows, blues and browns
That slant across their milk-white gowns.
A sleep-sweet wakefulness they drink
Inside their human cove, I think.

Housman's Subject

Perfect meter, perfect sound,
Perfect depth that seems profound -
Perfect stanzas, perfect verse -
Life is born beneath a curse -
All is fantasy and fiction
But the final malediction -
And probably that one as well -
For the pagan there's no hell -
Upon the ocean poets float
Each in a leaky little boat
As though adrift in Kafka's moat -
In his obsession Housman wrote -

My Death

When I die the sea will rage
And swells will thrash the rocks!
Stars will fall! The moon go in eclipse!
Volcanoes will erupt and spray their ash
And liquid red into the firmament!
All to tell the deity I died.
I think he wouldn't notice otherwise.

Strangers

I stare into a stranger's face
Until it is familiar,
Until I am at home.
But strangers pass
And strangers leave
And there is no way home
Except in memory.

Analogy

I plunged a dagger through my hand,
Impaled it to the table,
An artifact as natural as rocks.
And this - I said -
Is my relationship
To all of nature,
And nothing other,
Nothing more remains.
And I am not
Nor ever can be free.
Would my sensations
Were my sentiments!

Aristotle

Bagatelles about my life -
Quotidian - or poetry -
Merwin, Pound and Eliot
Don't threaten Keats' preeminence
Nor curtail or Shakespeare's
His longevity.
How long is fame?
Until the stone that holds the poem
Crumbles back to dust.
They only study Aristotle
Because he survived.
He did not survive
Because he was profound
But because no fire burnt the scrolls.

Robin's Poem

A soft little doggie
All fluffy and white
Sat by the river
And all through the night
He barked at the water
He barked at the stars
He barked at the shadows
He barked at the cars
He barked and he barked
Why this loud little pup
Even barked at the people
His barking woke up.

Epitaph

A man without a country,
A man without a god,
A man without a family,
A man without a soul -
Except the soul that permeates
The poesy he wrote.

5-5-12

Praise

A single thought of praise
(That is what he gave)
Can magically raise
Cadavers from the grave -

Keats' Self

Junkets was my deity -
My poesy his shrine -
Not born beneath an eastern star
Nor dying young divine -

No sense of self in poetry -
The stuff that passed the press -
How arbitrary, silly -
Heathens do confess -

So rigidly to disallow
A thought of self be said
Conjures up a special kind
Of magic - like the dead -

Picture

Lightly touched a verse is sketched -
Across the page a web is stretched
And gently lies, dusty, strange
In patterns that the pen can change -
Metaphors. What do they mean?
Pictures. And the sea has seen
More ghosts than rainy England's green,
Castles, battlements, a queen.

On The Ocean

Come with me to the edge of paradise
The sand, the rocks, the sea, the sea-gull's cry
Where loneliness itself is Arcady
And grey approves the color of an eye.
Let the sand replace with ocean noises
All the consciousness that's in your mind.
Let the echo of the grotto-cove
Be the only music your soul knows
Where hearing is remembered ecstasy.
Let the darkness of the sun-clouds soothe you
Gazing on the ever-reaching surf
Into sleepy pleasure. If a rain
Anoints the shore with sad and happy drizzle
There will come a mood that may remain.
The edge of earth is here, the edge is kind,
Encouraging with its own dismal care
Deep swells, soothing indifference, despair.
There is music where, calm after calm,
Swell after swell, waves follow each other,
And the even sea-horizon's distance,
All time and earth in one grey level line.
The inverse safety on this rock-shoaled shore
Is that in the feeling the shore beckons
Nothing matters. That itself is comfort.

The Temple

Symbol-met in a collapse of rhapsody
Hand-understood and sleep-embowered
In a temple of forgetfulness
That allows permission to be love
Beneath the arches of the time-raged sea
Out of storms and into other storms
Flower-laden, like a rhapsody
Where overhanging trees sway in the wind
And shed their leaves upon the ragged grass
Where statues open rock with rhapsody
The archives of the darkness and the rain
Are swept through deeper darkness upon stone
Still other darkness catches them, they pass
Succumbed to other waves of wealth and sea
And that mellow emotion, poetry.
Crack the temple open with a hand
And sunder it with sunlight suddenly
Like thunder in a lighted ecstasy
And leave them in a rubble of grey rock
Abandoned in the relic, reverie.
Beckoned, summoned, offered, Psyche moved
Among the leaves asleep, her body turned
Without undrowsing in her darkness-sleep
Enshaded in the shattered colonnade.

Rain

The plaintive morning rain
Against the window
Breaks legislation
No thought ever could.
My consciousness goes places
In my psyche
Where no sight ever went.
And my mind can see my person
With full impunity.

Defeat

You grovel, lie and sneak
When you're weak
And no one's on your side.
Like a cat,
Survival counts;
Not dignity or pride.

Made in the USA
Columbia, SC
29 January 2022